THE MANY TEARS OF A BLACK CLOWN
B. C. THE BLACK CLOWN

© 2020 by B. C. the Black Clown

All rights reserved. No part of this book may be reproduced, stored in a retrieval system, or transmitted in any form or by any means without the prior written permission of the publishers, except by a reviewer who may quote brief passages in a review to be printed in a newspaper, magazine, or journal.

Second printing

ISBN: 978-1-0878-6955-1

Printed in the United States of America

CONTENTS

Preface

CHAPTER 1

Home…Is Where the Heart Is 1
Mother 2
Something 2 Give 3
Look, Listen, and Learn 5
Oh My God 7
A Poem for Mama 9
This Is Why I Write 10
Real Love 13

CHAPTER 2

Ya Got a Few Seconds? 17
I Was Wondering 19
Remember Me 21
This Is What I've Found 23
When Will We Learn 25
Hey 26
Have You Ever 29
A Look at Life 31
This Is What I See 33
The Things I See Now 37
In the Short Time That We Are Here 41
In One Moment 44
Sign of the Times 47

CHAPTER 3

Stop 51
Slave 53
Instinct 54
If I Died Tonight 55
Stand 56
Hold On 59

CHAPTER 4

So I Guess 63
One More Day 64
Mend 65
Up the Creek 67
Was Love Too Late? 68
It's No Good 69
Let You Tell It 71
Love (A Fallen Angel 73
The Only One 74
The Users 75
You 76

CHAPTER 5

Sdrawkcab Backwards 79
Innocent? 83
Justice 85
When You Believe 87
From Where I'm Standin' 88

CHAPTER 6

I Wish 93
When Will It End? 94
My Last Tribute 95
Hold On to Me 97
The Things That We Cannot Wait to Talk About 98
Work to Help Others 100

CHAPTER 7

I Remember When 105
What We All Have in Common 107
This Is What Love Can Do if You Let It 109
What Do You Believe? 111
Why Not 115
I'm Sorry, Lord 117

CHAPTER 8

Love Is 4 Real 123
Ooh Whee 124
Piece 125
Who 127
Bend 128
Mothers and Fathers 129
Not Invisible 131
Our Fault 135
Pretty Picture 137
Sacrifice 138
The Rules 139

We the People? 140
Hope 141
In the World 2day 143
My Inspirations 144

PREFACE

This book is dedicated to those who were supportive over the last three years, and also to those who said I'd never find a publisher, let alone find an audience. When I first started writing the poems and songs in this book, I wasn't actually planning to put them all together in a book. Nor did I think that writing them would change my life and the way I saw it, mainly because I didn't think I could find any like-minded people who would buy it. But over the course of three years I did a lot of traveling from coast to coast, and I found that not only did other people like my poems, and felt the same about some of the issues that I address in my poems, but also through poetry, you can bring attention to a lot of social issues that many have no real idea about. Some of the subjects that are talked about are issues that we as a nation must take very seriously or otherwise we may find ourselves living in a "Mad Max" way of life.

Growing up, I was inspired by men like Dr. Martin Luther King Jr., who spoke to all those who had or were being mistreated in America, as well as many other places around the world. He wasn't just a voice for the blacks of America, but also for those who were not accepted as equals anywhere. He was more than just a minister; he was also a man who based his life around nonviolent and faith-based protests against hatred, and as a result, changed the lives of millions of his time, and many still yet to come. But what I learned most from him was that if you truly believe in something that many may hate you enough to do whatever it takes to silence you. In his case, it was one of the very people who he was fighting for and not the "enemy" that his civil rights movement was fighting against. But he was not afraid. He knew that sooner or later what happened would eventually happen. As a matter of fact, the day before he died, he gave a speech stating just that, and even said he didn't fear what was ahead. But even after his death, his message still lives on in the hearts and minds of leaders, even today, who still fight to make all men equal. I also learned that we can do so much more if we stand together in love and compassion, instead of returning hate and racism to those who did many evil things to people who just simply wanted to be treated as human beings, and not animals. In the short time that he was alive, he changed so much by living by example and not by just preaching to the masses. When I first heard the "I Have a Dream" speech, I saw how many faces not black were just as much a part of the civil rights movement. He was and still is an example of what faith in God can do. I believe that he also set a standard for Christians everywhere to live by putting our words into action so that all who do not believe may see our lives, and seek God. But I must say when I see how people treat each other, I have to wonder, did he die in vain?

I was also inspired by many musicians like John Lennon, Marvin Gaye, Bob Marley, and Eminem—John and Bob because they spoke of us coming together. One said, "Just Give Peace a Chance," while having a diverse crowd playing with him. And the other said, "Get Up Stand Up," to inspire us to stand for our rights. Both have become staples in music history because they weren't just entertainers. But many people have a negative image of them, mostly people who have never gone to one of their shows or who have never really listened to either. Marvin spoke to blacks about issues ("What's Going On") that are still as relevant as they were then. I was also inspired by Eminem, often known as a rebellious and vulgar rap artist, who speaks to the angry youths of today, but he's more aggressive than those before him in his way of expressing how he feels about a lot of the same subjects. But what they all have in common is that they all knew that music can cross lines of race or culture, and that, if we all come together, we can make a difference. And they also showed us that no matter where you're from, we're all the same.

I found out through these poems that age is not an issue and race is not an issue and geography is just places—places with similar faces, and that all people, no matter how they may seem on the outside, were all made the same. And that our ideals may differ but our hearts are just alike. Everybody wants love, respect, and compassion, but many are afraid to show these things, because if we do, many will take us as weak and vulnerable. Most of us don't even know why we're afraid. Most of us don't even care, because life has afforded the human race so many distractions and "feel-good" solutions that we don't see what we do to those around us and the effects. You always see in the media how someone is built up to be great, only so we can tear them down later to show that they are human, just like us, but then laugh at the Bible and all that it stands for, because we can't believe that we're not in control of our lives.

They say that history repeats itself, so what's the point of recording it, if we're only going to do it again? It is written that insanity is repeating the same thing, expecting different results. Does that mean our world is insane? I mean, there has been war since the beginning of man, because one wanted to control another or whatever the other one had one felt they needed it more. We record how many die each time and speak of how sad it was to have lost them. Yet, we still can't come together as humankind and help each other, as much as we would expect to be helped. Well, this book is a representation of what pain can turn into if you don't let it kill you. This book is also for any person in the entire world who wants to give up. I want to tell you, don't throw in the towel, as you never know what tomorrow may bring til you're there, and at any moment, you could be the one who needs love, respect, and compassion.

I've poured my heart and soul into this book, and without God and people He put into my life, I would never have made it. So I hope and I pray that these words take life and help to heal anybody who reads these words, and may it be a blessing in the name of our Lord Jesus Christ. And may we take notice for our children in the future because these are the last days, whether we believe it or not. I look forward to meeting you, and I hope you enjoy the book, my friend.

HOME...IS WHERE THE HEART IS

If home is where the heart is
Then mine must be lost
'Cause I call no place my home
But I still have a heart
Does this mean that my heart has no bounds
And no limits
So maybe it's the heart
That makes home
Anywhere?

MOTHER

Mother Earth is crying
Because the hairs she had
We build more and more houses with
For more people
Who are constantly
Killing and destroying
Everything in our paths
Mother Earth is dying
'Cause man takes
But never replaces
Because the system
That makes her whole
Is raped
And abused for our gain
At the expense of her pain
By human's selfish desires
And for our vanity
Soon our Mother Earth
Will be nothing
Without all of our love
She will die
And whose fault will it be?
(The selfish and money hungry warmongers)
Or is it too late
To save
Our precious Mother Earth?

SOMETHING 2 GIVE

If you're hearing
Or reading this
Then that means you've been blessed
With another day
And that should make you smile
And when you do that
You give someone else
A reason to be a little happier
And that is something to give
When you hold the door for someone
You don't know
You may meet that special friend
Or even just a good friend
And that is something to give
If you help carry something
And do this
With no expectations
It makes your karma better
And it also may restore that person's faith
In humanity
So when you think you have nothing to give
Remember that sometimes
It's better to give than to receive

LOOK, LISTEN, AND LEARN

Look at the world today
Hate is up
Love is down
A man says peace
And we attack his character
But yet we hail a man
Who wages war on a land
Because they believe differently
Than he does
Isn't that terrorism?

Or we hate a man
Who preys on little children
Yet we allow
Our children to be exposed
To violence and sex
What the media calls
Awareness?
And sexual freedom?
Hmmm?

We say we praise God
But hate our brother
And tell him how to live
As we die just like him
And put ourselves
On pedestals
Filled with pride
While our children
Kill
Steal
And fulfill prophecies

Look, Listen, and Learn Cont'd

We stifle our young
When we see them dream
By saying words like
Don't
Can't
And won't
And still expect them
To achieve
What we
Never have or will
And we tell them
Not to lie
Rape
Or steal
As we teach them how

When will we be FREE?
F = FINALLY
R = RELEASED
E = ETERNALLY
E = ENLIGHTENED
And when will we live
Humane as humans?
Woe to man
That claims that
The beasts and the fouls aren't civilized
After all, are we?
You get what you give
So what are you giving?

OH MY GOD

I met a man today
Who said that there's no such thing
As God
So I asked him why he felt that way
And he said,
"*I lost my wife and kids*"
"*I lost my job*"
"*If there was a God*"
"*Why has he taken all that I've worked so hard to get?*"

So I said,
"*You say you lost your family*"
"*Are they dead?*"

He said, "*No*"

And then I asked,
"*Was that the only job in the world?*"

He said, "*No*"

And I said,
"*Can you take it all back?*"

He said,
"*Of course not!*"

So I said,
"*Don't try and change what's already done.*"
"*Live for the now and don't look back.*"
"'*Cause what's done is done and what's to come isn't here yet.*"

A POEM FOR MAMA

My dear Mama, you mean so much to me
That it makes it hard to put into words
Just how much you have inspired me
To always be all that I can be
And you also always believed in me
Even when it seemed I'd never find my own way
You always knew that someday
I'd be okay, because you and Grammy always pray
Because your mother taught you what you know
Just as a good mother should
And she raised you with her love, and she gave all that she could

And in turn, you sacrificed all that you had for me
So that I could see, and be, all the things you dreamed I'd be
My dear Mama, thank you for loving me
Until I learned to love myself
And not try to love someone else
Like you love yourself
Thank you for teaching me how to persevere
And for making it clear not to fear but to hear
All the warning signs when danger is near

And thank you for the confidence to face the unknown
I've learned and seen so much since I left home
And all the people who I've met from coast to coast
You're the one I miss the most
So my dear Mama, this is my way of saying happy Mother's Day
From far away, and I pray that today is not the only happy day

THIS IS WHY I WRITE

This is why I write
Sometimes it's just to spite
Sometimes it's to show what's right
Often it's just to show God's light
'Cause if I never show it
I'm sure to blow it
If I don't say what's on my mind
Then I'll be like so many, blind
As they grow colder all the time
Because true love is so very hard to find

But hate is everywhere
In angry glares and stares
We are taught to beware
Because we're all so scared
So we stay always prepared
Often pushing away those who have cared

And we feel justified
By our pride
'Cause of those who have lied
We carry our pain deep inside
But what do we really gain
Other than pain
And stains
That drives us insane
And then there are some
Who play dumb
Or become numb
Or just run

To drugs, sex, and money to find peace
Or maybe just for relief
'Cause they can't release
Their demons and beasts

All because if we trust and believe
We are often deceived
By those we could never have convinced
And then we become relieved
When it's over and it's done
You're thinking, there goes another one
Who wasn't really a friend
Till the end
To be haunted and taunted
To be alone
WRONG!

We all hope
Some cope
We all choke
Some do dope
But what good is life if it's done in fear?
Or when you hear
Just what you wanted to hear
But fear makes the truth unclear
'Cause you're already sure of the end
And fear makes you a loser
Who will never win
Because of the past
Or the last

This Is Why I Write Cont'd

Remember as long as you get another day
At least you can say
You'll get another chance to try
To LIVE not die
We are always blessed as long as we're here
And no matter what happens, we have nothing to fear
And THIS IS...
Why I write!

REAL LOVE

Ain't it sad?
So many people go through life
Never ever really feeling loved
Because when they open their heart
It gets crushed by the very one
Who they gave their heart to

And ain't it sad?
That the amount of love that is received
Is often measured by
The amount of money given
The quality of the stability and comfort
And the degree of physical pleasures
And ain't it sad?
That if one doesn't get what they want
And when it's wanted, it's not considered real love
And ain't it sad?
That sometimes when one feels unhappy
The other isn't concerned
Because of something in the past

Well, the truth is, Love is…
Kind and patient
Love is never jealous
Not boastful or proud
Love is not rude or selfish
And is never quick tempered
It doesn't keep track of things thought to be wrong
Love rejoices in the truth, and not evil

Real Love Cont'd

Love is always supportive
Loyal and hopeful
And love never fades or dies
So if you find love that doesn't have all this
Well guess what
It's not love

I know none of us
Are really capable of this on our own
And maybe that's the reason
That the world is this way
But a man named Paul
Who at one time was full of hate
Believed and wrote of that kind of love
Because it was given to him
By his father
Who just so happens to be my father too
And if he wasn't
I wouldn't know love either
And wouldn't be telling you about it
So may these words
Guide you to our father
And may you know true
And everlasting love
As I have and many others have
And these words manifest healing
As well as blessings
Upon you and all who hear them
Forever

YA GOT A FEW SECONDS?

Well, the first thing I would like to say is…
Thank you for taking time out of your life
To listen to what I have to say
See the reason I stopped you was to share with you
Just some of the things I see
And I was wondering if you saw them too
Like we have people in this country who have so much money
That some would say more than GOD (how absurd is that?)
But they have so much
And so many have none
Why is it that those who have can't understand those who don't
Aren't all addicted and afflicted?
Or lazy or even crazy?

Some are ignorant and belligerent
But if the wealthy come in many shapes and sizes
Some are nice and some just aren't right
Why is it so hard to understand
That not all people without homes
Chose to be "homeless"
I mean, we've all probably said,
"Bad things happen to good people"
And have we all forgotten the earth is home to all of us!

Sometimes it's just easier to believe the worst and forget the good
So just as you gave me a chance to tell you what's on my mind
I just ask that if you could, maybe, try and find out a little about those who don't have
And if after you've gotten to know the how's and why's
Then maybe WE can heal our world

Ya Got A Few Seconds? Cont'd

Because our fear of each other is destroying us all
And we are, after all, family
So maybe we should act more like we are family
By giving a little time, love, and understanding
And loving one another the way we want to be loved

And may you be blessed
So you can share
You may just save a few
Broken spirits
Along the way

I WAS WONDERING

I was wondering
What should I do to be accepted?
Should I buy new clothes?
Or should I get a more acceptable hairdo?
Or maybe change the way I walk and talk?
I was wondering, what is cool?
Does it only depend on how much money I have?
Or do I need more education?
Or is it because I don't work hard enough?
I guess then, that makes me a loser…a failure
But if that's true…
By whose standard?
Does that mean that I can't possibly be happy?
Right?
WRONG!

My life is very fulfilling because
I'm alive and kicking
And because I can share with all kinds
Of people who would never actually know me
On a personal level but still know how I feel
Through the words on this paper
And every day I can make me happy
By making others happy

So I may not have a "J.O.B."
But still God always provides all that I need
Plus, I get to see if anybody thinks like I do
But best and not least
I AM FREE, to be
All that I want to be

I Was Wondering Cont'd

Because my God has blessed me with…
One more chance, one more breath, and one more day
And many more experiences
So I may share all that I can to help my brother man

So may you feel as blessed as I do
And may you be blessed more than me
So that you can share all of your blessings
With those who have less than you
Without worrying about what you may not have

REMEMBER ME

Remember me
I'm that kid who sat behind you
You know the one who you used to tease
Because you thought that you had more than I did
Well, I remember you
You were the kid
Who picked on everybody you thought was weaker
Well, you know
I hear the meek shall inherit the earth
But meek does not mean weak
It means the mild at heart
The compassionate
Just because you don't remember me
Doesn't mean that anybody remembers you
And whatever you thought about you that was so cool
Won't matter when you're fifty
I don't care if you remember me back then
'Cause you'll never forget me
Because of what I've become now
I'm here to tell you now
I'm not invisible

THIS IS WHAT I'VE FOUND

In this life, what I have found is
You are only what others think you are
Until you fail so they can make fun of your misfortune
And in this life, what I've seen is
Your friends can be your worst enemies
While they smile in your face
And in this life, what I believe is
We hurt each other because we're afraid
And no matter how much we often
Compare ourselves to others who
Think they are either better than us
Or below us, and why?
Is this truly our "human" nature?
Must we measure our greatness and success
Based on how others see us (even those we choose to ignore)
Does it really matter who has the most?
Can you take it with you?
No. You can only enjoy life to the fullest every day
And try to leave this world a positive legacy
For generations to come
May these words open your eyes and your heart
Because always remember you reap what you sow
And it could be you who needs love
In this life, this is what I've found

WHEN WILL WE LEARN

When will we learn
To be humane to one another
And not to be jealous of each others' successes
Instead we should focus on ourselves
When will we learn
That war only causes pain and suffering
That lasts for years after
Even long after we're gone
When will we learn
That the things that we do
In the presence of our young
Will someday come back to haunt us
When we see them do the same things
When will we learn
That you reap what you sow
So don't sow what you don't want back
Be a blessing so you can watch God's seeds grow
Then maybe we all will learn

HEY

Excuse me
Yeah, you with that cell phone
Are you just pretending not to hear me?
Oh, that's just my theory
Or do I just have you confused
With someone who gives a damn
About me
That little guy
Who you'll never know
Because of my hair and lack of funds
But wait, you'll be reminded of that every day
But still you'll say to me
Go away, go away
But can I ask you a question?
How do you think that you got that phone?
And you're not alone
Because of the people who've got no home
Who've got no jobs 'cause there aren't many
Even in the really big cities
Ain't it a pity that many
Have to live shitty
In this day and age
And get filled with rage
But who really sets the stage
As we all get played
Who is the victim, you or me?
It's hard to see
Who's really the enemy
But the truth of the matter is
We are just the victims of some sick game

Those who have power have used
And abused each one of us equally
So those who have
And those who don't
Have one thing in common
That in the end
We'll all meet the same fate
And all we all want is a little
Love in between
So thank you for your time
And I hope this little bit
We've shared was worth
The wait
Goodbye, new friend

HAVE YOU EVER

Have you ever had someone dislike you
Even before they got to know you
Have you ever been judged by the clothes that you wear?
Or have someone look at you with disgust?
Just because the clothes that you're wearing
Aren't made by some huge corporate name
With its so noticeable logo, that by its very name, says
Just how much money you have (or don't)
And that you spend a lot of money just to impress
A bunch of people that you don't know
Just so you'll be accepted into some so-called "in" crowd
That only cares about you because they hope
That if they have you around, they'll look cool too
And just like disease kills and destroys lives
Being popular is just another way that we separate each other
And have you ever been that person who went to a dance
But never got asked to dance
Just because you didn't really "fit in"?

Have you ever had someone say they loved you
But still they hurt you
Because of their own insecurities?
And why in our world today is it more common to be unhappy
With our hair, our clothes, our weight, our race and culture?
Who makes us feel that way?
Is it all in our minds?
Or is it because of the things we see on TV
And all other forms of media?

Have You Ever Cont'd

Are we all just victims of some really sick game
We'll always lose to?
Is the object for us to kill and steal from one another
Out of jealousy?
With unreal expectations of what makes us who we are
through materialism
Or is the goal just to destroy our faith in humanity?
We, as a society, have we become far too dependent
On a way of living that WE THE PEOPLE no longer control

Whatever happened to those days of need
And not just for vanity?
The bottom line is…we were all made differently
And none of us are perfect…and never will be
No matter how much
Or how little we have in this lifetime

So maybe instead of finding reasons not to like someone
Find reasons to love every person you feel smarter, prettier,
and richer than
There's someone looking down on you with the same disgust
And most importantly, love yourself
And the people you come across, 'cause you never know
When the shoe may be on the other foot
And you're the one looking up
After all, you've never walked in their shoes, right?

So don't be a blister
'Cause just as you don't want to be judged unfairly
Neither do they

Have you ever?

A LOOK AT LIFE

My hair is too long
(I must do drugs)
My clothes are too baggy
(I must be in a gang)
Well, that's the image that you created all on your own
And stamped on people like me (or who look like me)
Is it that my color is not what you like?
Too dark for you?
Would you feel better if I mimicked you?
Be a mirror image of you?
Be your follower, a clone?
Another sign of no individuality?

But what will you do if I don't do as you say?
Take my taxes…to spend on things that I abhor?
(Too late, we're already over budget)
And not to help those who you ask to die for our freedom
(Apparently not all,
Especially those who are worth a lot of money)
And send some of the greatest minds and hearts to war
For an undemocratic takeover…for land or oil
But it's all about control…right?

Well, the truth is…
None of us are above one another
Nor are we below one another
But side by side we stand (or fall)
As brothers and sisters

Look At Life Cont'd

The time is now—we can't wait
Because tomorrow's not promised to any of us
We're all just the same
After all, none of us will live forever…
So, for all those here now and to come
Strive to be a blessing to all who you come in contact with
As you want those around you to be
And you might just get blessed back because…
You WILL get back what you give out
Either way I know because…
I wouldn't be here if no one cared about me

THIS IS WHAT I SEE

To live the so-called good life
One must have a certain type
Of home, job, and friends
That are all a mirror image
Of what we want to see around us
To make them think that what they see
Is what they will get
All on the assumption
That you are somehow
A better person by the amount of crap
That you have amassed
And because all of it combined
Shows just how much money you have
Also how much that you are willing to spend
Just to say "I WON"
But what do you win?
And who has to pay?
Many waste their whole lives
To obtain so many frivolous items
That when they die they have to leave it
To irresponsible offspring
Who you never spent any "real" time getting to know
So you wouldn't know
They have a drug habit
Or that they just aren't very good with money
So after all your sweat and tears
All you have to show for it
Is just a bunch of crap that ultimately
YOU WILL NEVER TRULY OWN

This Is What I See Cont'd

So what's the big deal?
Isn't it sad that many won't even enjoy
The fruits of their labor
Until they become old people
And then they often try to love vicariously
Through their now adult children
Who now resent them for the time
That they put into their money and careers
Before their loved ones
All because we want to provide
A better life for them than we had
But instead of sharing the moments
They can treasure
We just have many
Wasted days and missed moments

Well, I'd like to think that life has to offer more
Than how much stuff we have or don't have
Time is precious and you can never go back in time
That only works in a fictitious Hollywood world
From the minds of people
Who have been put on a pedestal
So we can feel better
When we point out their flaws

Well, we all need things
For whatever reasons
But is it really worth it?
Are the sacrifices worth it?
So when you think about all
You have or what you don't

Think of those who you love
How much time you spend with them?
And ask yourself
Is it really worth missing?
Missing birthdays, recitals,
First steps,
And first words?

Money has its purpose
But it should not rule your life
And it can't be your God
But just a means to an end
Live life and never look back
Because you only get one shot
So don't blow it by not spending it
With the ones you
Love

THE THINGS I SEE NOW

Before I became a father,
I was an observer of things that happened to me
And I didn't have the responsibility of caring for anyone else
But now my life has changed
and I must now look at things from more than one way
For instance, before I became a father,
porno was just an addiction
Sorta like drugs, when you let those kinds of things get ingested
and it has an effect
And just like any other addiction,
it clouds your mind into believing it's not that bad
Until you see someone you love
have their life destroyed because of it
And because I'm a musician,
<u>I have to always be aware of what's out and who's listening</u>
But you seem to find that's really popular,
and you find that all they're talking about is…
How to get the girl you like
(have a fancy overpriced car and lots of jewelry)
How to talk to women
(calling them B***hs, H**s, S**ts, and Bustdowns)
And last, but not least
How to treat them (like pieces of eye candy…
making them feel inadequate)
And we can't forget you are only as cool
as all the junk that you can show that you have
Spent way too much money on, just so you can prove that
"HA HA, LOOK AT ME!"
"I MADE IT OUT, AND I CAN HELP YOU DO IT TOO!"

Things I See Now Cont'd

Not all those who do hip-hop or hardcore rap
do those things listed above
But those who do…they know who they are
There have been many great minds, hearts,
and souls to rise from the world's toughest ghettos
And there are just as many great minds behind bars
because we say things like…
"I gotta protect my hood,"
while allowing someone to poison our streets with drugs
"I had to kill him for our honor"
and do a drive-by that doesn't kill them but a three year old
And now that baby's gone,
you and your friends all get life sentences
All over pride that divides as it tears us all up inside
Are you listenin'…. This ain't a joke… Your life is at stake!

What I think about is why are so many children
being abducted and abused??
Every day, you turn on the news
and they report of another missing child last seen
In a public place really close to home
and not in a so-called bad part of town
And in most cases it's someone that the child knows
(a friend or relative)
It's not always strangers who do these horrible things
with little or no remorse
And they get the lightest sentences because the victim lived
Even though something that should
be their choice to give away
Was taken away before they had a chance
to appreciate how important it was

Why is the world so afraid to educate
the young minds of the world's future?
Because we're not gonna live forever
 and someday they'll be in charge
The PMRC protests a Marilyn Manson, Eminem, or Prince
But where was she when that girl in
The Dixie Chicks had her moment of shame?
America blew the Janet boob incident way out of proportion
Yet, Britney Spears can wear on a national network
something just as revealing
And what does America do—we buy into it lock, stock, and barrel
And tell our daughters we want them to be the next "Olsen twins"
While we condition them to be addicted to drugs by getting on
"Pharmaceuticals"
That we justify with "It must be okay because the doctor says it is."
But the scientists who do the tests on the lab rats are doctors too
And in order to advance the research in finding a "cure"
For any diseases or mental disorders,
there is a pill that can help us to control it

And when you can't afford those
you can always turn to street drugs
And if you look hard enough,
you can find one that gives that same feeling
But this "medicine" is against the law
and if you get caught with it, you'd be a "criminal"
So when will we stop treating each other like animals
and come together not just in tragedy
But to inspire all those who are here now
and all those who are to come

Things I See Now Cont'd

Remember God made all of us, and not just some of us
God doesn't make mistakes, He makes miracles
And every last one of us is one of God's miracles,
made in His image

So when we hate or destroy each other,
we show how we really feel about God

May these words anger and inspire all who read this
I pray that they share this with
all of those who have lost their faith

Amen

IN THE SHORT TIME THAT WE ARE HERE

When we are born, we come into the world with no expectations or dreams
And we come with nothing to give back, only our will to live
Some would even say
That to have a child is gift from God
Even if it's not planned
As a newborn, we have to trust
That the ones who brought us here
Really love us
And that they will always
Be there for us
Whenever we need them
Every day we try and soak up all
That is around us, the good and bad
So it's up to our parents
To protect and guide
And no matter how many books
On how to properly raise a child
Each and every one of us is unique
So of course no book
Can give you all the answers
So no matter what
We often have to go with our instincts
And the advice of those
Who have done it before us
Our parents and the so-called "pros"
But even they had to go through failures
Because life sometimes throws you curves
But often it's love and patience that

In The Short Time We Are Here Cont'd

Makes growth possible
And try as we might
We can't stop the inevitable
That someday this child
Will grow up and make decisions that
We may not agree with
Even sometimes boldly disobeying us
Because we did it when we were young
But as a parent we now start to understand
Why our parents got angry with us
When we chose the wrong path
Because of our natural curiosity
But instinctively
When things go wrong
We often turn to our parents
Even though the whole ordeal
Could have been avoided
If only we had listened to them
In the first place
But just like you can tell a child
What's hot and what's cold
Until they experience it for themselves
They'll never appreciate the warning
But that's just part of the human nature
Seek out firsthand what is unknown
Some people learn by others' mistakes
For others, that's just not enough proof
So we have to bump our heads
In order to truly learn a lesson
Even if our stubbornness causes pain

That could have been avoided
And no matter how much
Our parents love us
They can't protect us from
Everything

IN ONE MOMENT

There once was a man
Who lived by his plans
He had a big fancy house, fast cars, and a pretty wife
And he thought that was all he needed
To live a good life

And every day
He went on his way
But he was all work and no play
And he felt his life was okay

So every day he went to work he'd see this man
In tattered clothing begging for spare change
But he never stopped
Because he thought the man was running game
Never even thought to ask him what put him there
Just assumed it must be drugs or he was just a creep

Then one day he was heading home after a long day
And he decided to stop for a drink or two
And after about an hour or so
He'd pounded down more than a few
So he grabbed his keys and what money he had left
And went to his fancy car
He was sure he wasn't that drunk
And besides, he didn't live that far

He slowly drove out of the bar's parking lot
And didn't even notice a woman in his blind spot
She didn't even scream as he hit her
She just fell to the ground

But the moment he hit her
A large crowd formed all around
Still not knowing what was going on around him
He continued to roll

Suddenly, someone ran up to get his attention
Then reality took hold
As he exited the car, he was horrified to see
That he'd run someone over, so he started to flee
But someone stopped him
Then the police came

It seemed like a bad dream, like the kind you can't awake
Then he realized that it was all real and what was at stake
He was arrested and breath-tested for what he drank
But it was obvious he was drunk 'cause his breath stank
Now he's doin' time and
Has lost all that he had
And he knows he took
Another's life
And his life will never
Be the same and that
Makes him sad

No more house, car, or wife
So his victim isn't
The only one to lose their life
Now he realizes how
You can go from everything
To nothing at all

In One Moment Cont'd

As they say, the bigger
They are, the harder they fall
Now he's sitting in an eight-by-ten cell
With nothin' but time
Locked up, penniless
Without a dime
Just angry looks and
Deadly stares

So, just like the man
He so easily ignored and forgot
Who is free on the streets
In the same spot
But at least he's free
So you see
The moral to this story is
At any moment
This could be
You or
Me
In one moment

SIGN OF THE TIMES?

Everywhere you look, you are told
Lose weight to be liked
Dye your hair to look younger
Everything can be bought or sold
Or even if we choose to be drug-free
We're subliminally told we are sick
Mentally or physically
So instead of using illegal drugs
Many of us become addicted to what are called
"legal pharmaceuticals"
And those who use "street" drugs
are often ostracized and forever labeled
All because this is what we are constantly seeing on TV
And it is also what we're told in the music that we buy
Even the people who the media makes famous
Eventually become victims trapped by an image
So many of them just self-destruct
Because of the fact that they will never be
What everyone wants them to be
And then there are some things that our children are exposed to
That unless we are constantly watching over their shoulders
We can never be sure just what they see or don't see,
Even words that at one time were considered offensive
Crude or vulgar
Like B****, A**, and D***,
have now become words we hear on a regular basis
Soon the word F**k will be just like the rest
When will we change for the better
Instead of degrading and dehumanizing each other
How many signs must we see before we wake up?

WAKE UP!

STOP

Stop
Never
Wanna
Lose
Your
Image
Stop
Never
Deny
But
Try
2B
Alive
Inside
Stop
Being
Not
Afraid
Stop
Because
Your
God
Guides
You
Stop
And
Succeed
And
Love
In
All

Stop Cont'd

That
You
Do
Stop
With
No
Expectation
And
No
Worries
Stop
You
Are
Family

SLAVE

When you hear the word Slave
What do you think of? Is it a man or a woman?
What does a Slave look like?
Does a Slave have to wear chains and get whipped?
And when you think of a Slave
Do they have to be from Africa?
Of course not, why?
Because a Slave is anyone who is at the will of another
A Slave is someone who is told how to think, dress, and act
And is not truly free…so then, if that's true
Who's really a Slave?
Many give money away, even before they see their share (taxes)
Many can't say exactly how they feel or think (censorship)
Many work hard but spend more time doing their job
Than they do with the ones they love and doing the things
That make life worth living
All for the love of the dollar
Me, I go wherever my heart takes me ('cause I'm a hippie)
Whenever I wish (without fear that I won't get the things I need)
Me, and all of the money I make from doing what I love
I get to share with whomever I want, for whatever reasons (those in need)
Me, my time is always precious and joyously spent
So my question is, who's a Slave?
Come be free with me, 'cause life is short
And you can't take anything with you
It's what you leave behind (a legacy or curse of ignorance)
Don't be a Slave …break the chains

INSTINCT

Sadness
Is a way of the world
Gladness
Is for little boys and girls
Love
Is what we're all waiting for
Hate
Is just wanting more
I adore
Kiss me
Love me
Touch me

Instinct
Tragedy
Follows those who hate
Mad at me
From the pain you create
Let go
It'll never be the same
Oh no
It's all such a drain

IF I DIED TONIGHT

If I died tonight
What would the headline say?
Would it say I was a good man?
If I died tonight
Would my face be on the news?
In the newspaper or on TV?
If I died tonight
Would there be a day
Set aside and named after me?
If I died tonight
Would millions mourn?
Would many cry?
The answer is no
Because what have I given this world
Other than
My heart
My soul
My part
My role
I am not just a number
I am not just another statistic
I am—I am free!
No matter what I get today
Tomorrow I may have to give it away
Time is precious, so make the most of it
Go forth, my brothers and sisters
And multiply all of your positive
By passing it on
And may you be blessed abundantly

STAND

I've been inspired
By those I've admired
By those whose words burn like fire
With hope and desire
Like words from Martin Luther King
That to this very day make my heart sing
He said, "Let Freedom Ring!"
And "I Have a Dream"

Or when John Lennon would chant,
"Just Give Peace a Chance"
To unite all the races
In all of the places
Where ignorant minds
Commit horrible crimes

And Bob Marley called us to stand
Not to command
In another man's land
Why can't we understand
Our brother man?

And what about Elvis, he's put on a pedestal
Because he sang
And is religiously worshipped
Just because he has a famous name

Yet Marilyn and Eminem are rejected and disrespected
Or misrepresented and often resented
All because they stand
With legions of fans

And because they speak for those
Who don't have a voice
Or feel they have no choice
But to follow and conform
All that they abhor

Even from when we're born, we're torn
Between sitting or standing

So the question is…
Will you stand….or fall?

HOLD ON

My passion comes with great sorrow
My pain comes with memories of stains
And with nothing to gain
It drives you insane
Killing me softly with its song
But I just long
To do no wrong, so as long
As I can hold on
I'll go on
But destiny can't wait
For mistakes
Nor will it forsake
All that is in my soul
So I'll stay so ever bold
Just to hold on to my goal
And on to the truth
And my faith
So let go of the bad
And cherish the good
While you always stay positive
And you will be blessed
If you just hold on

CHAPTER 4

SO I GUESS

I used to feel that something had to be wrong with me
Because I have hopes and dreams I knew I could achieve
But that must just be me
At least that's all I've seen
People told me I was never gonna make it
Some just said, "Fake it till you make it"
But I keep telling myself I've got just what it takes
To open up those doors to get my big break
So I guess it's all up to me
'Cause only I see
What dreams mean to me
But they'll see, eventually
So till then
Where I come from it's so hard to show you shine
So many broken spirits often find they only end up getting high
That's all I've seen
And it makes it kinda hard to believe in your dreams

ONE MORE DAY

Sometimes I just can't sleep
My mind racin'
Often because of my failures
That I'm constantly facin'
All because I'm chasin'
The wrong desires
Higher and higher
On a tight wire
But I'm getting tired
Been lost in myself
Oh so much
I've lost touch
With who I am, but there's always tomorrow right?
In one moment
It could be good or bad
In one moment
I could be happy or sad
But I'm still glad
Just to see
One more day is okay
One more day

Sometimes I just can't face
Another failure or more mistakes
I just can't take
Any more shame
But who can I blame?

MEND

I feel like a stranger in this world
Like I don't really belong
I always get rejected, by all of the girls
And I just can't figure
Where I go wrong

All my life, I've felt all alone
Without a home
So I roam
It's all I know
Been some good times, and some bad
But I'm still grateful for what I've had
'Cause as long as I have my friends
I can mend

So many sad faces all around me
From the agony of failed hopes and dreams
Fightin' to make ends meet
Feelin' you've lost everything
As you're fallin' apart at the seams

UP THE CREEK

I've been searchin'
For what I don't know
I've sure been working
Runnin' out of places to go

But it's all done in vain
Just more and more pain
I've gone insane

I don't wanna be the same no more
Treadin' water closer to the shore
I'm on a sinkin' boat for sure
Up the creek, ain't got no oars

I'm a believer
Thinking everyone's got a heart
Always finding deceivers
Who have always got me fallin' apart

But it all ends in shame
Left always with nothing to gain
Are we all goin' insane?

WAS LOVE TOO LATE?

Over the years, I've had so many heroes
Many have come and gone
Most only live in my heart and dreams
But what they all have in common is
They all believed in love

So sad the greats are rare these days
And the worst is so abundant
Those who love are destroyed by hate
Was love too late?

A good man must suffer
A lifetime of sorrows to grow
But yet, hateful men spawn legions
By simply planting seeds
They all just wanted love

Was love too late?
To save us all?

IT'S NO GOOD

If love can make you hurt
Then why even try
It can make you happy
But it often makes you cry
And just because of chemistry
That doesn't make it love
You pour out all your energy
So you feel empty when you're done
I don't wanna fall in love ever again
'Cause I just lose, I never win
It's no good, it's no good
I pick the wrong one all the time
Good love is hard to find It's no good, it's no good
I see people every day
Who are just like me, livin' alone
All with sad faces
Dreading a lonely home
They wear disguises to hide
The pain inside
And pretend they're happy
As they feel so denied

LET YOU TELL IT

Well, I heard your version of what happened
Between you and me the other night
But I have to correct a few things that you changed
Like the fact that I was wrong and you were right
You must be intoxicated
Or inebriated, 'cause you're instigating
And now I'm debating
If we were ever friends at all
But let you tell it, it was all my fault
And if you tell it, you were totally innocent
But it's all lies, just a part of your disguise
I can see it in your eyes
But you'll deny
That you are wrong
But that's okay—we'll just let you tell it
You say you cared so much about me
But now you say you hate my guts and hope I die How can I believe anything I hear from you?
Because the story you're telling is a bold-face lie
So I hope you're happy now
And I hope you got what you wanted
'Cause we sure ain't friends now
Now I wonder if we ever were
But at least I know now and not later
And you can tell whatever version
You want 'cause I know the truth
And so do you, don't you?

LOVE (A FALLEN ANGEL)

She was so innocent when she was young
She even loved everyone under the sun
But now that's all done, 'cause now she runs
And now her problems weigh tons, or carry guns
No more fun for this little one
It all started, that very first time
She tried to find a love, a love that was blind
A man she could love till the end of time
One who made her heart to shine
But now she believes that's impossible to find
So she cries
For her love, her pain, and her stains
And she tries
Not to break, but can't fake or shake
What she's seen
And believed
Was love
She can't say how she feels anymore
'Cause all that she's adored
Or even explored or ignored
Are now becoming things she now abhors
As tears constantly pour

THE ONLY ONE

Well I remember when I was young
Things were simple, things were fun
Wasn't so many tragedies and there was hope
Wasn't so many people doin' drugs
Just so they can cope
People had their dignity and not just pride
Even made peace with enemies
Now loyalty is hard to find

But why?
Was it all a lie?

My first girlfriend was a lot of fun
When I first saw her
I thought she was the one
She had a sparkle deep in her eyes
But now I see, she was empty
Like me

But why?
Did I even try?

But it all works out
If we can just wait it out
But until that day comes
Just know you're not the only one

THE USERS

When we met, you said your word meant everything
But that was a lie
I bet you would have said anything
'Cause you had too much to hide
It's amazing how you pulled it off
How you had me believe it all
I opened the door and you fell right in
'Cause you know how to pretend

'Cause you're a loser
And an abuser
A soul consumer
All about yourself
I should have seen the look in your eye
That you're doin' what's true and your life is a lie
It's all about you
In all that you do
'Cause you're a user, thank God for karma

You warmed me up with a lil' favor
Just to throw me off
But that your flavor, a friendly neighbor
Look at all the friends you've lost
You must be crazy or just lazy
But in the end
You'll never rise
'Cause you wear a disguise with lies
Goodbye

YOU

I'm sorry I couldn't make you happy
I guess my love wasn't enough to please you
Maybe I loved you too much
But I'm just a fool, who wanted to believe
I should've known, we were never meant to be
It was just a dream
I know you probably don't even care
Just how much this time in my life means to me
And how badly I wanted and needed you
But now all I have is that old familiar feeling
And that's all, it was just a dream

(chorus)
I tried to hold you, love you, and heal your pain
But I'm not the one, all my love was in vain
But now it's over and there's nothing I can do
To save you from you

Every time I fall in love, it's never been true
'Cause it's always so one-sided
Either I loved too much or not enough
I'm starting to think true love is not meant for me
It must be time for me to wake up
From this useless and painful dream

Someday you'll see what you meant to me
And you'll never know what was in store
'Cause it was all about you, and not us
But thank you for showing me why
I don't really need love anyway
It was all just a dream, right?

SDRAWKCABBACKWARDS

Isn't it crazy
In order to get ahead
We often have to work hard and struggle
But as they say,
"We all have to start at the bottom", right?
But in order for a business
To run at its best
All parties should be happy
With most aspects of the job

And still the person who makes
The least amount of money
Also gets the least amount of respect
Like our teachers
Whose job is to mold and strengthen
Our young children's minds, hopes, and futures
Plus, they're expected to challenge them
And inspire them to be great
But most of them lose their fire
Because they have to struggle
Just to raise a family of their own

And what about those
Who work with the food we consume?
Many are considered failures and talked down to
And accused of not being smart enough
To get a "real" job (often attributed to laziness)
Which if that is true, then why do we trust them
With one of the most important responsibilities like…
Preparing our meals, which, by the way
Is one of the things that we all need
In order to survive, and if it's done improperly, it could be fatal

SdrawkcabBackwards Cont'd

But yet they are very often paid grossly inadequately
Without medical coverage
So that even when they ARE sick
They can't afford to take a day off or seek medical attention
So more people get exposed
While the big corporate companies make millions
Off the sweat of the brow of many people
They only see as a bunch of numbers

So it's sad that we trust them
With our lives, children, and food
But don't respect them enough
To give them just wages
So they can live the all-American dream
Instead of going through life wishing
To be appreciated and respected
And not have to have two jobs
That take them away from the very family
That they are struggling to take care of
But instead get to share
In those precious moments in life

And what about our police who are hated
They risk their lives every day for us
But instead of receiving love and respect
Just because there are police
Who abuse and victimize
Not protect and serve

But there is good and bad in everything
Even the bad ones WERE good at one time
They are here to protect us
From those who only want
To kill, steal, and destroy
Well, the bottom line is…
We ALL have struggles
So why can't we be more understanding
And respectful to one another
AND ESPECIALLY TO THESE VERY IMPORTANT PEOPLE
Because many of them do
The very things that many of us would NEVER do
And someday will be the leaders of our world
Or at least what's left, after we destroy it
And everything on it

So I urge you and anybody you know
To be careful who you call
A loser, failure, or reject
'Cause you never know
Who's gonna be the one on top
And who will be on the bottom
Who knows, it could be you
'Cause in this day and age
The term "job security" no longer exists
So even those who think that it can't happen to them
May be the ones eating their words
So just as the Bible says,
"The meek shall inherit the earth,"
Many of those being stepped on now

SdrawkcabBackwards Cont'd

Will someday be rewarded for their faith
So don't burn bridges
'Cause you can't cross something
That is simply not there

After all, we all have to share this world
And there's plenty of it for all of us
So let's stop going backwards...
And move forwards
To a better way of life
Never forget where you came from
Or you'll end up lost like so many
And that is truly backwards

May this poem be a blessing
To all who hear or read this
And always remember to love others
The way you want to receive it
Just say to yourself,
"What if that was me?"
And you'll find
It's much better to love
Than to hate... You choose!

INNOCENT?

The police and the judges
Are paid to protect and serve
A public that pays with their taxes
To see that the guilty get punished
For the things that they do to the innocent
But if that's true
And you're innocent until proven guilty,
Why do you need a lawyer
To represent you in defense of your rights
That, by the Constitution, we were ALL,
Not some of us, given by being a CITZEN?

How can one man speak for another?
After all, he can only speak
Of what he is told, whether it's true or false
And if you're innocent,
Then how can a man who
Commits a violent and heinous crime
Be locked in the same place
As a man who committed a crime
That only got him quick relief
From all of the pain (like doing drugs)
And he still gets subjected to the same treatment?

But if you're innocent, then there's nothing to prove
Because the truth is the truth
So if this country is truly
For the people, by the people
United we stand
Home of the brave
Then why are WE the victims
Of a system that WE the people created?

Innocent? Cont'd

And why are we destroying each other's hope for money?
But as the saying goes…
I guess we'll just fall (for whatever we are told)
And will never stand together as a nation
Because we're all so scared of the truth
And of each other
That none of us are really that innocent
Are we?

JUSTICE

Justice used to mean safety for those wronged
But most would say it's revenge
To make those who were hurt feel better
Who's wrong and who's right?
Some say justice is blind and tainted
By those who can manipulate
Our great magistrate
Scales are balance
Balanced by what?
I don't know by whom
But whomever it is
Should step down
To reality
Before justice kills us all
It used to be so safe, or so we all thought
We were all so trusting
But now we're seeing it's all about
Fear and money
And even those we trust do as they must
Tear all our freedoms away
Little by little, day by day

WHEN YOU BELIEVE

In order for most to truly believe
It must first be seen and experienced
But there is always the exception to the rule

So what makes it true?
Is it our perception?
But wouldn't that make it a biased truth
Based solely on speculation and not facts
Which leads me to this…

If you believe that, then it becomes YOUR reality
And not really the truth, but YOUR version of the truth
So when you believe
You truly can say, it's right or it's wrong

Like, for instance, if one man kills another
If that man killed him to save someone else's life
That can be justified
Because it was to save someone
But it still doesn't make it right
So maybe believing just isn't enough
Or is it?
Only YOU can decide

FROM WHERE I'M STANDIN'

From where I'm standin'
I can see for miles away
But into another day
But that's okay
For now
But right now is gone
So long…
So grow on
From where I'm at
I still can't figure
How some can say nigga
To another brotha
Who's not their enemy
At least not today
But tomorrow may be…
A different story

Or they could just ignore me
But we're one of many
To get no pity
In the many big cities
And from what I can see
I'm despised and denied
And sometimes
Feel alone inside
With no pride to hide
But still I'm alive

So just like everybody else
We live in…
Seconds
Minutes
Hours
Days
And years
But why does it often take
Until we're considered old
Before we choose to live
Our lives to the fullest?

Well, today
Is the day
To share and care
With those we love
'Cause we won't always be here
And time only moves forward
And doesn't stop
So we can't try again

So treasure every day
As if it was your last
'Cause it just might be
After all whatever you do today
Will be remembered
In days to come
Love + action = joy

I WISH...

If there was such a thing as
A genie in a bottle who granted me
Three wishes that no matter what they were
I would have to live with it
So, as many would, I'd wish the world would be good
That there is peace, and all wars would cease

My second wish would be to see the hearts of those I meet
And to have the power to heal, but still understand
How they really feel

Now the third, which is my fave, is how bad God wants to save
I want to die in His name, with His love in all of our days
But then I realized those were my wishes
To a mythical being, or should I say character
Is he God?
No…
So when you wish
Wish we all would benefit from your wish

I wish…

WHEN WILL IT END?

I began my journey years ago
And I still don't know where I'm going
I feel just as lost as I did then
Wondering if I'll ever find my destiny
Every time I think I've found my way
I realize that all I've ever done
Has just been part of a game I'll never win
When will it end?
I wish I could just give up
And walk away
But part of me wants to believe I have a goal
I know the devil's laughing at me
Because I'm still in this never-ending maze
Of the insanity of my own destiny
I slowly drown from my pain
And misery of never winning
When will it end?
In my human nature
I chase dreams I want to achieve
But all it brings me
Is never-ending failures
Am I cursed, 'cause that's how I feel
'Cause all I've ever wanted was
Purpose, hope, love, and peace
Never seeing any of them
Still lost like the rest
I don't wanna win
I just want to know

When will it end?

MY LAST TRIBUTE

I met you at the show last night
You looked at me like I had no right
To want to know just how you did
What you did to make you big
And how the ladies chase you down
And just how you got your crown
Even though your shine has gotten dull
I collected all the songs you've done
Been so loyal you'd think I was your son
Saw every one of your shows, even out of my way
Even losin' my mind slowly turning to gray
What more can I do to support
Any more than before
It all had began
This is the last, a blast from the past
Don't make me ask
Why you wore a mask
But this will be my last
Tribute to you, you lit the fuse
On my last tribute to you
Boo hoo
I've been teased because I encouraged you
Was told I should have discouraged you
But I just chose to be different than what you'd think
Because I still believe in dreams
When all seems lost in the cash
That always goes too fast again
Hold On to Me
Girl I wrote this song for you
Just to show my love was true
And to show you that I care
So you know I'll always be there

HOLD ON TO ME

And maybe you will see
Just what you mean to me

Hold on to me
Baby you and me
We're always meant to be
Just hold on to me

Time has passed us by for years
And I wanna calm your fears
That love is all we'll ever need
Just believe and then we will succeed

Hold on to me
And maybe you will see
Just what you mean to me

Hold on to me
Baby you and me
We're always meant to be
Just hold on to me

THE THINGS THAT WE CANNOT WAIT TO TALK ABOUT

When you watch the news, all you hear is how horrible the world is
And in those segments, they go into great detail of the tragedy
And even those that are shown,
it depends on what neighborhood it happened in
As to how many details will be told to the public

Yet, when you watch for the good news,
the bad usually outweighs the good
The news is told to you to make you feel either afraid or angry
Which is exactly what they want you to be,
so that people of all kinds
Won't want to come together to protest the unjust treatment
Of other human beings,
no matter how cruel or inhumane they may be

Like when we see mass tragedies like Columbine or 9/11
We all panic because reality sets in that none of us are immortal
And that we are all connected, regardless of race or culture

Why does it take such horrible events
for us to care for one another?
Why does it take so much mass pain
for the whole nation to come together in agreement?

Or what about Hurricane Katrina,
even that was portrayed by the press
As somehow related to race and economics
(as if any of that really mattered)

As to why the U.S. government was so lagging in the amount of
aid that was given

When we hear of tsunamis the whole nation is eager to help
But when it happens on our own soil,
we aren't so willing to take it seriously enough

Aren't we all Americans?
Don't we care what happens to other Americans?

All those who got out were those who had enough money
or the means to leave
Were those who were left behind somehow less important,
or of less value as human beings?
They pay taxes just like the rest of America
(those with jobs or who pay sales tax)

I see commercials about children starving in other countries
Yet I never see any about the families in America
Who are forced to live in housing
that should have been condemned years ago
Or even worse, how about the ones who live in their cars
Because they can't find affordable housing that isn't in a "hood"
That's infected with a booming drug trade
(that by the way the police can't or won't stop)
To me, this seems that the poor are being punished

WORK TO HELP OTHERS

I want to live on the edge of time.
A place I can be on nobody's mind.
Where there is nothing to lose or find.
And when I know what I want, out of the darkness I will climb.
I wonder sometimes if peace is the absence of conflict,
and if there is no conflict, is there no individuality?
And if there is no individuality, would anyone want to live?
If everyone had the same job and ate the same food and lived in
the same kind of house, what would be the point, and if everyone
had the same goals in life, would the world be a better place?

What if some of the greatest musicians would have "just dealt
with" living a "normal" life? What if John Lennon had said,
"After a year, if my music doesn't pay good, I'm going to work at
the grocery store down the road? And I will sacrifice my heart
and my soul, so that my wife's parents will accept me as family."

How is it that people can watch people perform a play at the theater,
or we can listen to someone sing a song on the radio,
or even buy the next Harry Potter book,
but when we see someone close to us trying to do the same,
we reject them.
Is it because they suck at what they're doing?

I don't believe that at all. I believe it's mostly because we can't see
ourselves making it and so we hold everyone else to the same
guidelines that we used to get to where we are. Because that's
where everyone else belongs, right?

Well, I know I don't want to be fifty years old and working a dead-end job at Wal-Mart. I don't want to live in a trailer in the middle of tornado alley. I don't want some overpriced, too bling, bling, gas-guzzling vehicle. I don't want to show off what I've done in my life with a bunch of unnecessary belongings.

I DON'T CARE IF MY FORKS MATCH MY SPOONS! I want to enjoy my life as much as possible, with as many people as possible, always. And I don't know how to do that by spending all my money on things I don't really need. I get more joy by getting something for someone who can make it possible for them to help others. I would rather donate $20 million to genetic disorder research than spend $50 on a car that makes me look "well off."

And I want to give without expecting it back. I only expect those I help to help others. I believe if we would help each other more, without holding it over their heads, we all would be better off.

I know that if someone gave me the sewing machine of my dreams at a value of about $400, and they never expected anything back from it, I would, on my own, give back at least double that to watch them do it for someone else.
Just because they supported what I was doing and wanted to help, not because they wanted me to do something for them later, and not to boast of what they did to make themselves out to be "better" than me.

I know people help each other, but they should do it for the right reasons. So I guess the point I'm trying to make is,
"Don't shoot the twelve point buck just for the rack on the wall, but for all the people you can feed with its meat."

I REMEMBER WHEN...

When I was young, the word respect meant something
We were taught to respect even those who didn't respect us,
and that in order to get respect, you must first give it

And there weren't organized street gangs because parents were
allowed to be parents and not live in fear of being punished by a
system they pay taxes to (that pays the salary of those civil
servants) whose pledge was to "protect and serve" and not make
us feel that we're the criminals

And back in those days to hear of something bad happening was
just something that happened to other people in so-called bad
neighborhoods

Back then, a nosey neighbor was a blessing—we just didn't know it
And now we complain about our youth of today that's running wild
At one time, Elvis and Jim Morrison
were considered to be evil and too sexual
But now you can turn on any station
and what they did would be considered tame
Where did we go wrong?
Many people just want to blame our government
Some blame our schools and the frustrated teachers
(who are grossly underpaid)
And our police have to eke out a good living,
even though they risk their lives each day,
only to be told they need to do more
More what? No one can agree on how to get rid of all the drugs
and dealers

I Remember When Cont'd

And what about the children who we lose to the street who never had a positive role model…? Who do they turn to?
The teacher who has the responsibility of molding minds that don't want to be molded but instead are filled with rage instead of hope

Or what about a policeman who became an officer to protect his family, only to find out that most of his so-called friends are the ones who he will someday have to put behind bars

There was a time that the prison system was only for those who took whatever they wanted
And now they're filled with people who just simply lost all hope—hope of a better life, hope that someone will lead them to something other than a habit they can never afford, an unwanted or needed child at sixteen, to opportunities that don't lead them to a stay at our local "Department of Corrections"

I'm starting to think that it was all just a dream, or just a myth?
I guess when Martin, John, Bob, and Cesar died, so did our hope
Those days are gone…but I STILL REMEMBER WHEN…

WHAT WE ALL HAVE IN COMMON

It brings me to tears
to see the sadness on so many faces
Because the society that we live in
is based on others' views of us
And that sometimes
can make it almost impossible
to see the true us

Some people never even get a chance
to act how they want to
because of fear of rejection
And with rejection comes
shame and LONELINESS…and separation

And if you ask most people,
"What is your biggest fear?"
Some say, "Death," or "What I'll leave behind"
(And to whom will they leave it, and how will they spend it)
Or maybe it's just the very idea that WE ALL will
someday soon die that really scares us

And some would even say, "It's because no one really loves them,
because everyone they've ever loved doesn't love them enough or
the same"

And it brings me to tears
to know that so many children see more
HATE
than
LOVE

What We All Have In Common Cont'd

But isn't that backwards?
After all, WE ALL want to be loved and respected
We want to be wanted
And need to be needed
Well, GOD wants you and loves you
And needs you, WHY?
So He can show others
His love, His patience, and
His guidance
Because you get what
you give out
So always give your best
for all

You just gotta
seek and believe
And you'll receive

And remember
that in order to live
you have to give
from your heart
in order to receive
from the heart
And may your life
be blessed abundantly,
as well as ALL you
touch

THIS IS WHAT LOVE CAN DO IF YOU LET IT

Love is a beautiful thing when you're alone
And when you find someone it makes you feel special
Makes you feel that anything is possible
It makes us feel alive,
so alive that we trust someone other than ourselves
And that makes it very easy to be blinded to all of the signs that
tell us if it's really love

And even if it's not real from the one who we love
We often just brush their behavior aside, thinking that we can
make them love us
The same way that we love them,
even when their actions tell a different story,
Still hoping that as the saying goes, "Love conquers all"

And because we see it in movies and videos,
Many think that it's really like that in real life…
and are often crushed
When they find out that all that they had believed about someone
Had all been a lie
So after feeling betrayed we're embarrassed at the fact that we
once loved that person and they didn't feel the same
So some take the shame upon their hearts
Vowing never to love again just because of the last experience
That didn't work out for whatever reasons
But we often feel it was our fault not theirs,
feel like we should or could have done more
To save something that was obviously not meant to be,
otherwise it would be
But the truth is…life wouldn't be life without the good
and the bad

This Is What Love Can Do If You Let It Cont'd

Instead of focusing on what could have been
We should focus on the good things that came out of it
Some people never even get that luxury
of even finding someone at all
Think of those who died young
Or those who lost a loved one to a tragedy,
And feel blessed to have at least had the chance to say,
"It hurts, but I'll live"

So in the times that we hurt the most, we learn the most
And we can cherish the times that we don't

I pray that this heals those who believe that they can't go on

Just remember tomorrow's not promised
And yesterday is already gone…so live, love, and forgive
Or you will never heal
And you'll carry that pain, and infect others with your pain
Don't be a virus—be the cure

WHAT DO YOU BELIEVE?

I've been told that the Bible was written by men
and it's designed to control and brainwash
Evolution says that we all come from apes
and there's no God—He's just like everything else,
manmade
But either way, we all have a choice of what we want to believe
to be true or false
and we also make choices by the things that we see,
and how we view them

So if that's true, then when will the apes take over?
We say that we're more civilized, but we can't stick together
They live in the jungle and only kill to protect or eat
But humanity wars with one another for money and land
Yet, there are many species of apes in all varieties
but they can keep from hating each other out of jealousy
And most importantly, they don't destroy their Mother Earth

If man is the most civilized being on the planet
Then why is there racism, because of color or culture?
Why is there hate when we're all supposed to be sisters and
brothers, or those we don't know considered to be others?
And none of us would exist without a father or a mother

Yet, it is so hard to believe in God, who, by the way,
Has done something no man could ever do
And that is to bring us together even in tragedy
And through faith, hope, love, and trust
And if there's no God, then what's this life for?
Are we just wasting time? Or do we have a purpose?
We spend our whole lives looking for answers, why?

What Do You Believe? Cont'd

We can't even agree on evolution or divinity
But yet to destroy each other is logical?
Why does it take great tragedies to get us to see our obvious
mortality, as we have millions who die every day
We study all the things that kill us, and even find cures for some,
yet we all die

And if the Bible was written solely by man
And faith is also created by man, then ask yourself this
Why do all religions say
That we should love one another as we love ourselves
And not to love money because we can't take it with us

Also the Bible urges us to treat all people with compassion
Even when they hurt us
And tells us that none of us is perfect, so we should always be
humble
But many of us think that's just too hard to believe
Yet the very apes that we are told that we evolved from
Are provided with the things they need to survive,
without question
Do they worship material things to make life worth living?
But who puts who in a cage? What's really an animal?
And these days even humans (inmates, convicts, lifers)
are sentenced to live and die in cages to be forgotten

And as we build more houses, we build more prisons
And as if that wasn't bad enough, we medicate our children
'Cause we can't control them,
but we get mad when they become addicts

So I guess what I'm saying is…who made you?
It's up to you to choose whether you wanna win or lose
But either way, you can't live forever and tomorrow's
not promised

So what are you doing today?
Being an ape without a jungle?
Or a believer in love, hope, and happiness?
I personally hope you choose not to be a monkey's uncle
But instead, be humane and not an animal to fellow humans
'Cause He's patiently waiting for you
Just ask, seek, and believe
Before your time is up, and it's too late

WHY NOT

Imitate
those we see on TV
Mistake
what's wrong for what's true
We take
our lives for granted
We feel
our solutions are in dope
Some play
with others' feelings
Many lose
faith, hope, and desire
Can't fake
laughter for their pain
It's time
we all believed
Our loss
Without God's grace, life is tougher
Emulate
those we wish we could be
Partake
in things we know we shouldn't do
We break
the hearts we're handed
We kill
each other's dreams and hopes
Some stray
from God's loving healing
Many choose
to end their lives when times are dire,
and can't take

Why Not Cont'd

rejection and shame
If we allow our minds to continue
to be deceived,
the cost will be
that we will continue to suffer

We find it's easy to have faith in people
but find it hard to have faith in God
But how many of them would give their only son for you?
If you don't believe
Why?
May God speak to you and everyone who reads or hears this
Can you say that Jesus is your savior?
If not…time is ticking, don't get counted out
May this be a blessing upon you

I'M SORRY, LORD

I'm sorry Lord
I can't love them like you love me
I can't have the patience
you've always shown me
From your loving grace, through your loving son,
when will you release me
from my unforgiving and tormenting flesh
so that I can have peace, within you and your heaven?

I'm sorry Lord
that I'm so weak
and because I'm afraid of the words
that you need me to speak

And I'm sorry Lord
that I've always had fear of loneliness
and for having more fear of being lonely
without a wife or family
than I have ever had
about being without you to comfort and heal me
And still I stray from your way

I'm sorry Lord
for following my own selfish desires
Am I insane, 'cause it usually ends up in pain
with nothing gained

I'm sorry Lord
I dream of fame and fortune to help me feel alive
as I watch others die every day inside
I

I'm Sorry Lord Cont'd

'm sorry Lord
for being so resistant to you
and not listening to your warnings or your requests of me
I'm sorry Lord
that I often take my eyes off of YOU
in search of love and foolish pursuits
until you gently rebuke
But still you carry me through
You clear my eyes so that I see the truth

So I'm sorry Lord for all that I do, against you
And I just wanted to say, thank you, for loving me
more than I could ever love you

LORD, YOU LIFT ME UP

I think back to the times I tried to hide
all the painful memories that I held inside
And while I struggle with my flesh
indeed I must confess
Lord you picked me up and gave me rest
So I'm blessed
You see me fighting with my inner man
and the Holy Spirit
You know I'm just a man
You know I'll never hear it
The world has smacked me down
Yeah I've been around,
always down to clown,
trying to show I'm down
But when the world has rejected
the words I found,
you know I'll always have the strength
because I'm heaven-bound

Lord you took my rage
out of a steel cage
and placed me on a stage,
and now I've been saved

Lord you lift me up

CHAPTER 8

LOVE IS 4 REAL

I wanted to love you
More than words could say
But you wouldn't let me
You just pushed me away
Away, well okay
Then I'll just go away

Love can heal
Love can make you feel
Love is everything
We are searching for
But it's gotta be real
And baby my love is for real

I know you've had some pain
But I'm just a man
It really drives me insane
'Cause I can't understand
To make it go away

I said I loved you
That wasn't enough
I tried to show you
But that wasn't enough

OOH WHEE

Ooh whee
That way she makes me feel
It's so unreal
I just peel
Out my skin
And begin
To let in
Emotions unfold
I seek just to hold
But lose control
Of my feelings
From the ceiling
I'm reeling
But finally at last
I'm past, so fast
What a blast Ooh Whee!

PIECE

I know that you're watching
My every move
And I bet that you're thinking
Or hoping that I will lose
But I am determined
To be the best I can
'Cause I'm not a quitter
And that's just the way that I am
Why can't you see
That you're hurting me
But helping to make me see
That you're my enemy
Trying to steal my steam
While chasing down my dreams
But no matter how hard you laugh
And no matter how hard you grab
You can't have a piece of me

I know that you're plotting
All the time
Cursin' and wishin'
I'm constantly on your mind
You try and discourage
My confidence
To make me believe
That misery is my friend

WHO

Constantly in competition
Pointing out our inhibitions
Making the wrong decisions
With cruel intentions
Not to mention
Cutting emotional incisions

Who's cool?
Who's a fool?
Whose rules?
I just wanna know "who"
Don't you?

Is filling all our minds
With nothing but lies
In so many kinds
Of interesting disguises
It'll be our demise
As Mother Earth rapidly dies
Until we live each other's lives
Or can stop our own
We should just accept one another
Until we change ourselves
'Cause the "who" is me
The "who" is you
And that's the truth

BEND

Many read the paper, but never see the news
Maybe read of capers, but never real issues

But they don't really care
Do they?

Lots to talk about, all about big names
What's it amount to, just about the games

Mister, mister, can you see
What the future will be
Now we will see
If it all will end
Won't you come and bend

I've never really wondered, never really dared
I've never really bothered, why should I even care?

And they don't listen
To me?

Let's talk about all the hurt you've caused
Let's talk about all the lies you said

MOTHERS AND FATHERS

Mothers and Fathers
Are Kings and Queens
They hold a high position
As they encourage our hopes and dreams

Mothers and Fathers
They set examples and enforce our rules
And try to protect us
So that we won't live as fools

Mothers and Fathers
Have been through some of our pain
But often forget what it's like
While we drive them insane

Mothers and Fathers
Love us when we don't know what love is

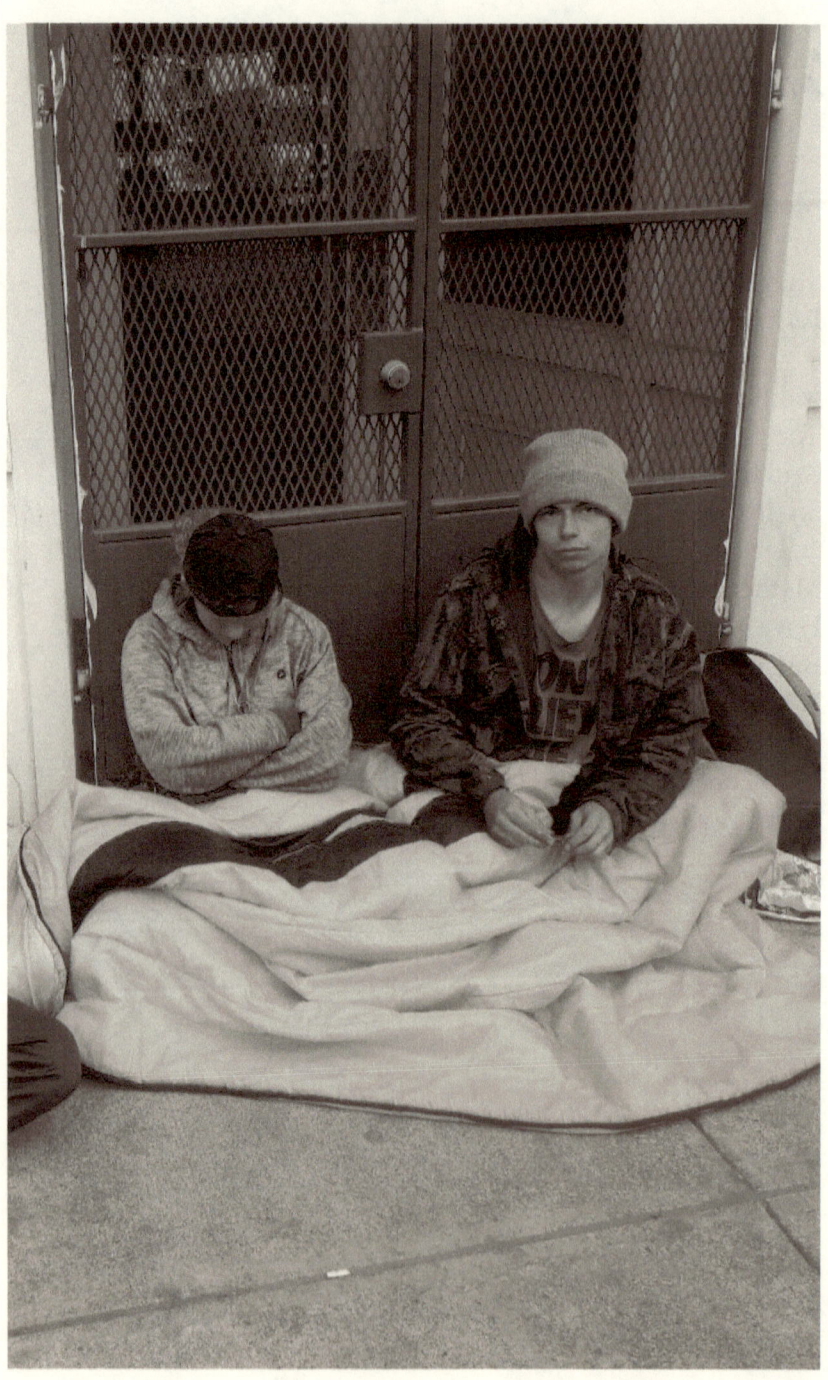

NOT INVISIBLE

I am human just like you
I breathe, I bleed
We breed with greed

Yet, we as people, even though we're equal
and all of us eventually die
We fight one another, as we become consumed
And fear that we're all doomed
To fail worse than those who were alive before us
As we are constantly measuring ourselves
against images of those around us
By what we have or don't have
Or if we will or we won't
Make it or fake it
While wearing many faces, trying to hide traces
Of the things of our pasts,
hoping never to have to go through it again
Many people are suffering

We walk past those who we see,
who don't even have a place to call their own
Yet we boast that we are the richest country in the world

Like Tupac said, "We got money for wars
but we can't feed the poor"
And many would say all Tupac was, was just a thug
Whose spirit lives on in millions of hearts
Who actually listened to him, almost religiously
But because he spoke the truth,
he was assassinated over greed and jealousy

Not Invisible Cont'd

The Bible is the book published in the most languages
And is in more homes than television, internet, and newspapers
Yet many say that God is not real
because of what we see in the world today
But the Bible has been around longer than any of us
And has prophesized all that we are going through
Still many are surprised that the war in Iraq, like many wars,
was foreseen and written about

Yet most think that we are there because of "terrorism"

But who are really the "terrorists," us or them?
Some have even compared Iraq to the Philistines,
who God gave David victory over
Well George W. Bush is not David…nor did he achieve what
David did
And his fight hadn't been blessed a
nd many soldiers lost their lives

I commend everyone who went to war…
and I pray that many will come home
So their offspring don't have to be like so many other generations
Growing up without a parent and not really understand why

We who believe that Jesus died for us,
it is time that we stopped being afraid
And instead unite and show the world that God is real
And the only way is to show love like Jesus
to those who are suffering
Instead of building bigger and better-looking churches

We should do our part,
just like all the soldiers who gave their lives
To fight for people who they never met
and for all those who they love here

We are in the last days, "Every knee shall bow,
and every tongue shall confess that Jesus is Lord"

I'm writing this because God put people in my path
Who showed me His love
Even though I gave Him
No reason to do so

OUR FAULT

I was watching a television show
that though the intent was to shame young girls
into changing their promiscuous behavior
no one really cared that
they were lost, lonely, and felt unloved
just like so many often abused and angry
teenagers seeking attention
by any means available at the time

And the parents are blamed for their behavior
even though they're working all the time, to provide for their families' needs
so they couldn't be there
to do what a parent is supposed to do
to not look or seem irresponsible

And so the only role models these kids see
are on TV, America's cheapest babysitter
or worse yet
molesters, pedophiles, addicts, and other victims
who are preying on their need for
attention, acceptance, and what these girls think is love

In every instance that I read about
the common denominator was they all needed guidance
they just weren't getting

No one person is responsible
We all are because vulgarity and sex is the norm
and things that are good aren't what are popular

Our Fault Cont'd

I think it's a shame that it's easier to blame
than to take time to prevent these children
from self-destructing
I think we should teach them by example before it's too late,
instead of making fun of them, which will only make them
more rebellious

PRETTY PICTURE

Nobody's perfect
But you are what you are
No matter what others might think
And as the saying goes
You get what you give
And all you do is take

You got everybody fooled
'Cause you wear the right clothes
Know the lingo
But you're really a fake
It's all a pretty picture
That's not really you, is it?

I wish I could take back
All the time, energy, and love
I wasted on people like you
Who drain the realness of everyone around you
Because of your fear
That if you show who you really are
We'll know you're empty

SACRIFICE

We're taught that if we want anything in life
we have to sacrifice
but at the same time try to stay true to your heart

We're taught
you'll always have more friends
on the way up, and very few on your way down

So a lot of people
never have a positive understanding
of what sacrifice is
But to really sacrifice means to give,
not just give up

Jesus was a real sacrifice
because he died for people
who scoffed at God,
even after He gave His only son

But we can't sacrifice our pride and so-called honor
Well, I'm grateful
that God thought my soul was worth His son's blood

So what sacrifices have I made?
Only God knows, right?

THE RULES

Should humans
be judged because of the color of their skin
Or should they be judged
by the character that they are, deep, deep within?
But that is against the rules
Can't we just accept
without contempt?

Could I love you
without having any expectations,
just be there
whenever you need me, with no limitations?
But that is against the rules

WE THE PEOPLE?

The United States of America
United = unity, meaning we are together
States = people, meaning a large amount of humans
America = society and community, meaning us
This country was built on diversity
And many people shed blood on this soil
So how can we be so racist?

Capitalism, ain't it grand?
But it doesn't seem to be working
Homeless are ignored (though many are veterans)
in this country
But we'll go to war
and lose some of our best
to liberate countries
that hate us
and would kill our young

Thank God for our brave soldiers
because they love us enough to go
even though many die every day
And how does the civilian world
thank them?
We don't
So are the "We" in "We the people," the United States?
How much more blood do we need to shed
before we are the people again?

HOPE

My mother says I could sing before I talked
And even says I wanted to run before I walked
I must have known that life was short
But I'm still not sure what this life is for
I see sadness whenever I go anywhere
And it seems sometimes no one really cares
Hope, it's all that we live for
Hope, can make us feel alive
Hope, makes us want more
Hope, is what makes us try
And keeps us alive, inside, hope
Dreams are something that pushes you to succeed
They help you to appreciate everything you see
So when times get tough, and you can't get what you need
Or when the world just seems so mean
I see pain wherever I go
And without hope, it will surely grow

In the World 2day
In the days we live
Pain and suffering are front-page news
The evil is winning
Leaving all the good people
Jaded and used

Back when my mother was a girl
There wasn't as much fear in the world
And if one of us fell
We'd stand together to catch them
But the world has changed
Take a good look

AT THE WORLD 2DAY

In the days to come
Drug pushers will be convicted and addicted will die
And more young will lose their innocence
Way too soon
In their short lives

MY INSPIRATIONS

I see sad faces
in many places
in all of the races
catching felony cases

All because of their mistakes
they miss out on many breaks
while being loyal to friends
who are fake who teach us to learn to hate
But some people stand out without fear
to face being hated or revered
And because they have big dreams
they fall victims to jealous schemes
that often discourage those destined to be great
into believing mediocrity is everyone's fate
But this is a poem, for all the clones
or for those who feel alone, and continue to roam
because so many have gone cold
and are waiting to die as they grow old
and most of all, for those who answer the call
against all odds, we will never fall
You're either a hater
or a congratulator
But only you can choose
if you will win,
or will you lose?

These are my inspirations

ABOUT THE AUTHOR

RALPH TUNSTELL is a writer, poet, and songwriter from the Midwest. I have been traveling and playing music since I was 12 years old. My mission in life is to bring people together. Through music and other form of art. Also writes short stories.

www.ingramcontent.com/pod-product-compliance
Lightning Source LLC
Chambersburg PA
CBHW020829020526
44118CB00032B/411